MW00476531

Eros
in Autumn

Haiku, Close to, and Other Short Poems

Steven Schild

To Ted —
MAY you find something
here to enjoy.
[signature]

Up On Big Rock Poetry Series

SHIPWRECKT BOOKS PUBLISHING COMPANY

Raising independent publishing to the level of indie music & film

PO Box 20
Lanesboro, MN 55949

IN®
DIE

Cover design by Shipwreckt Books
Cover photo by Steven Schild

Perfection of Shadows was selected as one of fifteen haiku to be displayed in the Poetry Parking Lot, Lanesboro, Minnesota.

Suddenly Summer

Suddenly summer
dies; leaves lament its leaving,
blaze in their own blood.

A Second in September

Young girls in autumn
glisten by sweet as fresh-cut
flowers falling down.

Eros in Autumn

Eros in autumn:
Old men admire young women
for what they once were.

Autumn Leaves

Still beautiful,
they hold on long as they can;
then fall has its way.

Love Song: A Lamentation

Birds do not sing
to the wings that bear them
or eagles to the air
that carries them
to places they did not know
they could go.
Lungs hum no lyrics
to the ether that fills them,
nor do hearts drum hymns
to the blood that wills them
almost endlessly on.

And I do not sing
to what I every day see,
which makes it so clear,
my dearest of dears,
that it is oh, so wrong,
that for oh, so long,
you have heard no love song
from me.

Autumn Air

Someone burning wood;
death-watch trees hold up a sky
tentatively blue.

Colors

Ferocious red
bleed fall's final roses, fierce
yellow sing their blues.

Simile #3

What could be colder
than the walking-stick taps of
a blind man in rain?

Simile

Incongruous as
the Dostoevsky scholar
carping about cold.

Above Any Grave

The women we lusted for
are in wheelchairs,
or, if not,
they creak along
like cracked boards,
their pants fitting
like tarps over loads of hay.
And the men,
the men long lost
to the men they once were,
wheeze along behind
with bellies big as planets,
prostates big as bagels,
outsized only by
the dreams
we all once had.

And yet
when I watch that old man
help that old woman down the hallway
and whisper in her ear
softer and kinder than
sixty years ago anyone dreamed
he could or would or would need to,

I know love's bloom
lasts longer than,
is stronger than,
the stone above any grave.

Do This in Remembrance of Me

How the pecker leapt
when she swept to his embrace:
I too once was young.

Seated Female Nude

Her thighs are too big
and her breasts are too small,

their destinies
to balloon and fall,

but she doesn't care,
not at all,

so there she lounges,
there she sprawls,

undraped, unguarded,
open for all

to ogle, to stare at,
to study, to see

the essence of us,
the creature we be.

The Old Fornicators
(with apologies to R.H.)

He creaks, she canters
the same leafy path,
he in wrinkles of no distinct shade,
she in luminous yellow top,
glistening blue bottom,
pony-tail tantalizing
side to side in rhythms
in sync with what drove
her thighs and once did his.
Thirty years ago he could've
caught her, in the right light
caught even here eye,
but now he falls unnoticed
further and further behind
fueled by the smolder
of an old man's fire,
driven by what stays,
this lingering desire
in whose embers still reside
what once would've put them
side by side but now leave him
shadow to her effortless stride,
shadow so deep
that it never does die.

Old Man Crosses the Quad
During the Dog Days of August

What to do with my eyes
amidst this welter of thighs?

Two Takes on Strangers Encountered Circling the Lake

i.
Her chocolate thighs
churn side by side—what a ride
would be like on her
bike.

ii.
All the rights parts in
all the right places, the best
her electric smile.

A Rhyme about a Rump

My,
oh,
my,
muttered I
as the barely clad
waitress
slinked by.

Nearby
what caught my eye
was the one-time bunny's tail,
still spry but not as high
as it once did rise,
for no matter how we try
we cannot defy
what looks us straight in the eye –
the gravity
of those years
gone by.

We've no choice but comply.
Why,
oh,
why?
Heavy sigh.
My,
oh,
my.

Sailor on a Separate Sea

What sort of man
might I yet be,
a sailor on
what separate sea,

the past an odd
antiquity,
what's left,
perhaps,
the best of me,

or, better put,
the test of me.

Manhattan Tourist Staring Through a Cab Window on a Rainy Morning

Wonders of the world:
In Paris or in Podunk,
breasts bounce just the same.

Burka

Cover all you can
but beneath that shapeless dress
all of you is there.

Concerning the Commotion Caused
by the Stieglitz Photos of O'Keefe

What's shocking
is that we were shocked
that the photos
showed pubic hair,

and that all it takes
to shock us
is to show us
what we are.

Left in the Sun

As if things could last
I turn window-ledge photos
away from the sun.

The Perfection of Shadows

Truth in black and white:
the perfection of shadows,
changing with the light.

The Price We Pay

What faces the sun
must fade, this the price we pay
for living in light.

Sunshine and Shadow

Even on bright days
we live near darkness because
sunshine sends shadows.

Morning View, Lake Winona

Sunlight on water—
too many sparkles to count.
Not a one will last.

Upon Marveling at
John Whelan's Figure Drawings

Nook and cranny,
crease and crack,
imperfection,
budding fat,

slope of belly,
small of back,
upper arm,
its graceful track,

bend of elbow,
arc of knee,
fractals,
concentricities,

length of leg
so languidly
sprawling there
for all to see.

Just a figure drawing,
lines upon a page,
the artist is an old man now,
the model fat with age,

just a figure drawing,
a rudiment of art,
just a figure drawing,
a sum of all its parts,

and yet, these lines add up somehow

to something more than that,
for here the charcoal seeks and finds
humanity, intact.

In Line at the Confectionery

Best of the sweet treats
at the candy counter is
her scrumptious rump.

Morning Sweet Roll

Maybe her hair is still wet
because she just lately
scurried glistening from the shower
after staying in bed not to sleep
but to wrestle and ride with her husband
like she was eighteen again,
willowy and wanton and wanting
and animal horny and now
sated
and hungry in a different way
and pleasant as breeze
over first coffee,
which she draws from the cafeteria decanter
while doing me the favor
of small talk and a smile,
not knowing that I sweeten my black coffee
by sharing the sugar from
her morning sweet roll.

Exchanging Dirty Looks

When your V-neck dives
to places I would love to,
how can I not look?

Waitress at the China Buffet

Not enough skirt there
to cover all that's there, so
feast, you old eyes, feast.

Young Women's Bodies

Young women's bodies
    nearby nod "Come hither" to
        old men's delusions
           old men's memories
                old men's sweetest dreams.

Cruel Eyes Don't Look

Cruel eyes don't look
at older women passing
for what they once were.

Concerning the Young Couple
Come Home for Lunch

Let's hope for their sake
it's a nooner brought them home,
let's hope for us all.

Woman on Stairs, the British Museum

The curve of her hip –
as fine a piece as any
on display that day.

Bald Bohemians

Bald Bohemians,
their berets cocked at the slant
of suns sliding down.

Impossibly Close

Impossibly close
to perfection the way she
wields her wondrous ass.

Her Face

Beauty and sadness,
two petals of one flower—
who am I to choose?

She once was a Pretty Woman

She once was a pretty woman
buxom and beckoning,
cataract of hair cascading
to nearly you know where,
and that smile,
that smile held me tighter
than her sinewy arms when once
we did dance slow.
That was years ago.
Now she lives at the end of a nearby lane,
children grown, marriage blown,
living room tidy as a museum,
lawn perfect, grass groomed as if
for a ceremony
about to begin.

I saw her this morning waiting
for a light to change,
I passed right in front of her
on a four-lane road,
but she couldn't tell me from the billboards
holding up the horizon; her eyes
were blank as the blacktop between cars,
wearing no expression but rush-hour dour,
bearing no evidence of anything
but the way the world wears us down,
the way a smile falls to frown,
the way the sky hits the ground.

She behind the Counter

Brown as a berry,
lithe as a rope,
just a glimpse of her
gave an old man hope,

hope about hoping,
hope about dreams
no matter how crazy
or hopeless they seem.

Friendly Waitress Chats up an Old Patron

Not invisible,
nor truly a man, either.
It's sad, and it's so.

Things in the World Fallen Down

A silo beside Highway 14
just this side of Dover;
a stack of stones,
alongside steps,
toppled over;
a star from the sky;
a tear from an eye.

Son Walks Through Dead Father's Barn, Remembering

Gunny sack, clevis,
two-man saw rusted clean through—
what I knew is gone.

Upon Seeing a New Poem
from Richard Wilbur

The old man still writes,
about spring, no less, singing
in the sights of death.

Tao

All I have written,
it is my tao to say, will
like wind blow away.

Good Luck Lasts

This gorgeous day
makes this lucky man wonder
how long good luck lasts.

The Book on Johnny Callison, Gorman Thomas, et. al.

Some years like the Babe,
then to journeymen they fade:
This game breaks men's hearts.

Baseball Fan Bitter about the Strike Year

So angry that he
never saw Santana pitch:
this the price of hate.

To the Blonde Stranger

Her bounteous breasts
are her burden, the weight of
always being watched.

Found Pressed Between Pages

Fathoming passage,
her letter is in pencil,
her love is in time.

Post-coital

Then it is over.
Sated, we lie naked in
what is yet to come.

Children

Like crystal they glow
and may shatter so, thus this
cruel truth we know:

Love's never enough.

For Such Women, #3

The eyes still dance
like a girl's, crow's feet
be damned.
Her smile has lasted,
lost no luster
through decades
gone, through
children born and grown
and died and gone.

Hold my hand, honey;
I shall never forget
the way it felt
all those years ago,
the way it led me here
and keeps me here,
the way it still warms me so.

Solitary Dream

I can't be long, love,
from your hair, your hips, to your
solitary dream.

Still Breaking Hearts

Women loved him,
and how could they not
with that face, those hands,
that smile, those lips
that knew so much
but never said a word
about the ways he'd known them.

But now,
once-hard belly sloped to paunch,
dancing eyes sitting this one out,
sun-brown skin seeming too long
left in the sun,
with all that was inside him
and behind him
going against him,

we regard him in repose
and remember him once and for all
for all he once was,
for all he still is,
still breaking hearts.

Nothing Matters More

Nothing matters more
than love, or so we say when
sunny is the day.

But when pain courses
blood-thick through our veins, will our
bright resolve remain?

A Nickel's Worth

The sky, the sky
can't be that blue,
and the clouds
are too lovely
to ever be true,
and as such it is so
that I never shall know
a nickel's worth
of the how or the why
once such as you
would love one
such as I.

Irreconcilable Differences

Pretty as could be
was the crystal till it crashed—
some things can't be fixed.

Nearly November

The cold weight of rain
convinces late-autumn leaves
to give in, let go.

Imaginary Lines

The line between
blue and green,
black and grey,
night and day,
sky and sea,
you and me.

Following Rain

Drops cling to clothesline,
on the edge of their seats to
watch the rainbow show.

Gathering Stones
(for Joseph Tadie)

Even crude stones shine
when sun strikes them so as to
find our eyes open.

Bedside Digital Clock

Our evening ended
at 10:53
when she went to sleep
and I went to pee.
But, oh, such a fine time
we had until then –
two old folks living
like young folks again.

Illuminati

In the store mirror
the shock of what we've become:
Such sadness light brings!

Sam Saw a Rainbow

Sam saw a rainbow
in granite sky, just desert
for an upturned eye.

Going Bald Badly

Going bald badly:
incorrigible wild hairs
losing their last stand.

Autumn Evening

Autumn evening:
Day's colors blinding bright, and
just as dark the night.

Skyline in Silhouette

Ascending darkness,
church spires spear night sky's blue skin,
but beauty bleeds through.

Iceberg Sky

Fall trees bleed color,
wordless birds fly, dark clouds skate
on an iceberg sky.

November

Deep-throated dogs bark;
raw wind snaps like lynching rope:
Fall is here, and fear.

Night Sky, November

White sliver of moon –
such thin blue you can see through –
may this never end.

Full Moon on Snow

Full moon on snow; no
clouds, no darkness in sight, no
end to endless night.

Lake City Awaiting Winter

All the boats are gone.
The blue water misses them.
Gulls glide by and sigh.

Upon the Long-Delayed Conviction and Sentencing of a Holy Man

Fallen from on high,
he walked in the world wounded,
chastened, chastised, free.

Watching from Above

Smiling ear to ear,
safe in the stone's cool shadow,
a gargoyle conspires.

Woman Walking to Work in Late Winter

Cold wind plants
an April kiss
on this lone woman
going to work
another day,
a touch long gone
and now it comes
this way,
tearing at
the hair she tried
to hide under her scarf,
chilling to the bone
the pale, frail frame
shivering
under an old overcoat.

They say spring
will ride in on this wind,
they say tulips
will rise from
the crying snow,
they say
how pretty
it shall be;
she wonders when
it will feel that way,
when this cold will let her go,
will feel more like the hand
of a husbandman
than the hide of a gigolo.

The Nun in Her Habit,
the Priest His Long Robe

i.
The world as it was:
How I love it, how I wish
it once again was.

ii.
The world as it were:
How I love it, how I wish
it ever had been.

Lament from One Stall Down

Young man's urine stream
roils the still water while I
whiz wistful and slow.

Outside Ed's Bar

Young people in tight pants
and tight skin and thickets
of hair,

young people who smoke
and inhale deep and don't
worry, not about that,
not yet, anyway;

I nurse my one drink and get ready
to amble home; they bolt back
one of many they will not count
and wait like a wet kiss
for the coming of dark.

Skimming the Obits

Skimming the obits:
second-hand heartbreak on this
ordinary day.

Good Old George Borer

Like stone in a quarry,
he didn't stand out;
like grass in a meadow,
he was not one to shout.
But he loved both his children
as he loved his one wife
and he lived as one should
with one's only one life.

Gone all too soon
will be good old George Borer.
The world should've known
to take notice before.

From a Funeral

"Peace be with you," rasped
he who beat his sons bloody,
hiding in God's house

from this gospel truth:
Absurd the word of the Lord
in the world We made.

At a Funeral Home

Blur in a mirror—
scent I can't place—no one near—
the dead are still here.

Keepsakes

Keepsakes clog closets,
full of our foolish wish to
keep what we cannot.

Around the Lake

Lonely as a priest
he circled the placid lake
searching for a sign.

Old Men outside the Library

Chalky bones challenge
steep marble steps, so moved by
the smell of old books.

These Old Men Know Things

These old men know things
but we ignore them like wind
whispering secrets.

Aging Iceman's Glare

Aging iceman's glare,
Messier's menacing stare—
young stickmen beware.

Father and Son, Old Men and Young

How close they came to
mayhem, legs locked, arms entwined,
fighting to a draw

and then letting go,
fearing to look further for
what they dare not know.

Variations on a Theme

Son sings through midnight;
his sleepless old man listens,
strums the same guitar.

Ancient Battles

Ancient battles,
fathers, sons,
never over,
never won.

Carnal Elves

My, my, the glint of that thigh
on the old man's clouded, shrouded eye,
and the reverie of how and why
such deluded dreams
might drop true from the sky
as if a gift from carnal elves:
My, but these old fools
know how to fool themselves.

A Walkway Where

Tall trees side by side
canopy a walkway where
no one passes by.

Feeling an Eminence Fade

Two tufts of grey
on a gorgeous spring day,
two old, old men
who while walking away
were passed by young women
whose hair snapped behind
and dusted off memories
of how body and mind
had borne eighty winters
and not worn away
but brought them instead
to this beautiful day
when they felt in their hearts
and they heard in their bones
an inexorable ending
that could not be
their own.

After All That

Crow, on a tombstone,
takes a shit; after all that
life comes down to this.

It is Sure to Come –

It is sure to come –
the budding, the bedding of
the last erection.

Marker

Why granite, marble,
such hard stone, to remember
flesh that is so frail?

Concerning the Inability of Haiku or Any Poetic Form to Do Justice to that Stunning Slip of Flesh between Her Navel and Her You-Know-Where, Exposed beneath Sweats as She Stretches While Yawning

Tell that story true?
No truckload of syllables
has any chance to.

To a Young Woman

You make this old dog
wish he were once again wolf,
hunting from hunger.

The Way I Want to Go

May my heart explode
with me in full stride chasing
what I hope to catch.

About the Author

Steven Schild was raised on a dairy farm outside Houston, Minn. He lives in Winona with his wife Margaret; they have two grown sons, Jake and Sam. Schild has published poetry in a number of literary magazines and anthologies and has won awards for his poetry from Viterbo University and the League of Minnesota Poets.

Made in the USA
San Bernardino, CA
21 November 2014